D1543625

gardening with
containers

TORONTO
BOTANICAL
GARDEN

This book has been presented to the
Weston Family Library

By

Joan & Alan Lenczner

Valued Sustaining Friends of the
Toronto Botanical Garden

2008

gardening with
containers

George Carter

photography by **Marianne Majerus**

RYLAND
PETERS
& SMALL

LONDON NEW YORK

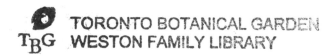
TORONTO BOTANICAL GARDEN
WESTON FAMILY LIBRARY
TᴮG

First published in the USA in 1997,
this edition published in 2001 by
Ryland Peters & Small, Inc.
519 Broadway
5th Floor
New York, NY 10012
www.rylandpeters.com

Designer **Ingunn C. Jensen**

Project Editor **Toria Leitch**

Production **Kate Mackillop**

DTP Manager **Caroline Wollen**

Illustrator **Michael Hill**

American Consultant **John E. Elsley**

Text © 1997, 2001 George Carter
Design © 1997 Ryland Peters & Small

The author's moral rights have been
asserted. All rights reserved. No part
of this publication may be reproduced,
stored in a retrieval system, or
transmitted in any form or by any means,
electronic, mechanical, photocopying,
recording or otherwise without written
permission from the publisher.

Originally published as *Containers.*

ISBN: 1-84172-174-3

Printed and bound in China

10 9 8 7 6 5 4 3 2 1

contents

Growing plants in containers, like all gardening, is a compromise between nature and artifice. It offers the opportunity to simulate all kinds of growing conditions, place plants wherever they are wanted, grow combinations that would be impossible together in the open ground, and overwinter tender plants under cover. Container growing also makes it possible to rearrange the outside look of your house in much the same way one might rearrange the interior—to radically change its seasonal appearance, or transform a terrace for a different purpose.

The projects in this book do not just look at the conventional container; there are ideas for portable plant screens—the equivalent of hedges in container gardening—for architectural containers, and for the plant pot as gate pier. The designs not only show how to grow in containers but also suggest how to place plants in an overall garden or back yard design.

In addition there are new suggestions for transforming an ordinary window box, terra-cotta pot, or wooden tub—simple changes that make containers relate to their setting. This is gardening as exterior decoration as well as horticulture.

George Carter

terra-cotta

There are many variations in the color of terra-cotta, from the harsh red of new machine-made pots to the softer texture prevalent in hand-thrown pots. The 18th-century landscape gardener Humphry Repton used pale stone paints and lime washes to disguise the terra-cotta exterior, allowing for a wider range of planting plans and locations.

above A hand-thrown urn painted dark green quickly patinated to a mottled bronze color. Planted with pinkish-blue hydrangeas, this urn looks best displayed above ground on a simple painted wooden plinth.

above center The tall and distinctive shape of these pots is emphasized by their white painted exteriors, which read better from a distance than darker terra-cotta.

above right Magenta-colored pinks with silvery-green and gray foliage make an effective low mound of color in early summer. Dianthus prefer sunny conditions; place them near a window or door where their sweet scent can be fully appreciated.

right This large terra-cotta-colored pot has been planted up for early spring with dark blue and white double hyacinths. Make a simple bold statement by placing it in an open space where the outlines and colors stand out.

right A painted wooden stepladder makes an effective staging for the display of pots and can be especially useful in small gardens when the need is to go up rather than out. Change the plants seasonally, or simply fold up the step-ladder and store it away after the plants have died off. This late spring display includes felicias, marguerites (*Chrysan-themum frutescens*), drumstick primulas (*Primula denticulata*), and double daisies (*Bellis perennis*).

below Clipped box (*Buxus*) is an invaluable container plant since its effect remains the same throughout the year. Here an underplanting of pink and purple petunias gives the box a colorful border during the summer flowering months. You will need to liquid feed this arrangement during the growing season to keep the petunias going, in the face of competition from the box.

above center This variegated hosta (*Hosta sieboldiana* 'Frances Williams') is contained in a wide low urn-shaped pot which suits its spreading habit. The bold architectural foliage of hostas continues throughout the growing season, making it an attractive plant even after the flowers have died off.

above right Machine-made terra-cotta pots have been painted in white, gray, and blue latex. The color combination and design on the larger one conjures up the delft flower pots much used in 17th- and 18th-century gardens to stand in rows on walls and terraces. Choose plants that sit comfortably with the color of your painted pot.

right Dwarf tulips make a very good spring plant for this simple terra-cotta pot. The larger varieties may need staking; use ordinary canes or hooped willow supports. The double early tulip 'Schoonoord' shown here is a good short white flower for containers and will provide long-lasting flowers in April.

patinated terra-cotta

Many modern terra-cotta pots, especially machine-made varieties, have a raw new look that can detract from the effect of an attractive planting plan. They can also look out of place next to old containers that have been softened with age. One answer is to tone down new pots using special paint to simulate patinated terra-cotta. In this project we show how to artificially age a terra-cotta trough using this method, and then how to display it effectively side by side with naturally patinated pots.

materials & equipment

terra-cotta trough 24 x 9 x 9 inches (600 x 230 x 230 mm)

2 naturally patinated terra-cotta pots with 10-inch (250-mm) diameters

small pot of off-white or gray oil-bound distemper

small paintbrush

scrubbing brush

bucket

pot shards

20 quarts (20 liters) soil-based potting medium

*3 bunches creeping soft grass (Holcus mollis 'Albovariegatus')
in 6-inch (150-mm) diameter pots*

2 box shrubs (Buxus sempervirens)

painted pots

Painting terra-cotta pots is a useful way of introducing vibrant color to an ordinary pot. It also disguises the rather harsh looking red appearance so prevalent on modern machine-made pots. Use the colors chosen here or pick your own combinations to match the architectural background of your garden. To create the greatest impact paint the pots in simple, striking designs, and pick plants to match the overall color scheme.

materials & equipment

machine-made terra-cotta pots: 2 with 9-inch (230-mm) diameters,

2 with 7-inch (170-mm) diameters, 2 with 6-inch (150-mm) diameters

1 quart (1 liter) each of yellow flat latex and palm-green flat latex paint

masking tape, 1 inch (25 mm) wide

paintbrush and watercolor brush

pot shards and 30 quarts (30 liters) general purpose potting soil

10 lilies (Lilium reinesse)

10 creamy osteospermums (O. 'Buttermilk')

6 lime-and-cream petunias

grouping terra-cotta pots

To achieve a satisfactory grouping of plants in pots requires planning. Stick to one material to give unity, but choose a variety of sizes and shapes. Mix textures and scales with seasonally changing flowers (see project for planting suggestions). Pick a plain background for a visually complex group, or a more decorative one for a simple bold display.

materials & equipment

large pot, 14 inches (350 mm) high with 16-inch (400-mm) diameter

medium pot, 10 inches (250 mm) high with 10-inch (250-mm) diameter

basket-weave pot, 14 inches (350 mm) high with 14-inch (350-mm) diameter

container, 14 inches (350 mm) square

small pot, 7 inches (170 mm) high with 10-inch (250-mm) diameter

very large pot, 16 inches (400 mm) high with 18-inch (450-mm) diameter

small cylinder, 12 inches (300 mm) high with 14-inch (350-mm) diameter

small shallow pan, 15 inches (130 mm) high with 12-inch (300-mm) diameter

large shallow pan, 7 inches (170 mm) high with 18-inch (450-mm) diameter

pot shards, manure, and potting soil (see steps, opposite, for different types)

bamboo canes, garden ties, and spiral-shaped wire frame (optional)

left A shallow glazed ceramic bonsai trough makes a useful container for a low planting of impatiens; keep this plant well watered as shallow plantings are more likely to dry out.

below This 1930s shaped urn, because of its simple outline, makes a good centerpiece that will hold its own against a complex background. Here it is planted for summer with blue solenopsis.

masonry Stone or marble

containers, unless old, are difficult to find today athough they are still made in Italy to traditional designs. Cast concrete in various stone colors is more commonly found; paint smooth surfaces in lime wash or distemper and allow more porous, pitted surfaces to patinate naturally.

above Oriental glazed ceramic pots offer very good value and are usually of simple and elegant shape. They are also available in blue and white, which looks very nice outdoors. Space them out on a terrace or parapet as a repeat element.

left Lightweight fiberglass-reinforced concrete containers are useful for roof terraces or where containers need to be moved around. Here, one is planted with a barberry.

above A cast concrete trough looks best patinated or distressed to complement the asters. Encourage moss and mold by painting with liquid fertilizer and keep in a damp, shaded position.

above left This container has been cast to look like an 18th-century water cistern and has been treated to resemble lead. The pink of the hydrangeas is a good contrasting subject.

left A concrete basket-pattern pot of early 19th-century type echoes the basket-edged beds and actual basket planters often seen in Regency gardens. This sort of pot looks good raised on a low brick wall or wooden pier, displayed with pink geraniums.

below A simple glazed ceramic pot makes a good foil for a rather visually complex pelargonium. These plants have a long flowering season and tend to spread out in a random fashion.

vertical planting

Town gardens quite often need privacy, and one way to achieve this is to plant upward. An ordinary hedge is one solution, but even on a roof terrace one can achieve more interesting screening effects using containers. This project shows how to get a banded effect of pleached lime underplanted with ivy, below which are containers for flowers. If you wish to enclose all the sides of your garden, simply add more troughs and trellis backing.

materials & equipment

2 concrete troughs 24 x 18 x 18 inches (600 x 450 x 450 mm)

1 concrete trough 18 x 18 x 18 inches (450 x 450 x 450 mm)

dark green flat latex paint

section of trellis, 6 x 6 feet (1.8 x 1.8 m)

2 vertical wooden posts 84 x 2 x 2 inches (2200 x 50 x 50 mm)

coated wire or garden ties and sea-washed pebbles

pot shards, soil-based potting medium and slow-release fertilizer

1 red-twigged lime (Tilia platyphyllos *'Rubra')*

6 ivy plants (Hedera helix)

8 white petunias

white trailing and purple verbenas (Verbena tenera)*, 8 each*

2 ferns (Athyrium filix-femina)

planting plans for urns

Urns are particularly prevalent in Italian gardens where they form an integral part of the architecture of the garden. They can be used effectively to punctuate a design or, standing alone, to create a focal point; place them at intervals on walls and balustrades or display them high on gate piers and plinths.

materials & equipment

shallow "campagna" urn

pot shards

soil-based potting medium

plinth for display

*10 houseleeks or hens-and-chicks (*Sempervivum tectorum*)*

*bear's breeches (*Acanthus mollis*)*

Cordyline indivisa

*lemon tree (*Citrus limon *'Meyer')*

trailing Lobelia

brickwork trough

A tall brick planter creates a strong visual impact where an urn or a smaller container could not. This provides the opportunity to create a stunning display of flowering and non-flowering plants, which are nevertheless simple enough to appreciate at a distance. The trough can be used for a mixture of permanent structure planting and seasonal bedding out, so it can be used to create a display that acts as an important focal point in the garden all year round.

materials & equipment

small bag cement, 100 lbs (1 cwt.) aggregate, 50 lbs (½ cwt.) concrete sand for concrete foundation

105 frost-resistant bricks (Old Cheshires have been used here)

small bag cement, 100 lbs (1 cwt.) mason's sand for mortar

wheelbarrow, bricklayer's trowel, pegs and string, and level

1 piece 18 x 18 x ½ inches (450 x 450 x 10 mm) exterior-grade plywood

4 concrete blocks 18 x 9 x 4 inches (450 x 230 x 100 mm)

30 quarts (30 liters) potting soil

1 half-standard rose (Rosa 'Sanders' White Rambler')

4 Hebe pinguifolia 'Pagei'

18 tobacco plants (Nicotiana alata 'Lime Green')

circular pipe with flowering tree

In a paved garden or where soil is not available, large shrubs or small trees can be grown in broad concrete pipes—an inexpensive way to contain soil and display plants. Here a decorative niche gives height to the arrangement and frames the cascading flowers of the fuchsia plant with its frothy mass of underplanting.

materials & equipment

section of concrete drainage pipe to fit plant, 20 inches (500 mm) high with a 36-inch (900-mm) diameter

dark blue-green flat latex paint

pot shards

50 quarts (50 liters) potting soil

slow-release fertilizer

weeping fuchsia (F. x speciosa 'La Bianca')

10 lady's mantle (Alchemilla mollis)

6 pelargoniums (P. 'Friesdorf')

shell-faced trough

A quick and simple decorative treatment refines the appearance of an ordinary concrete garden trough. Aluminum leaf adds a shiny surface to the shells but any metal leaf looks good, the most extravagant option being gold. Blue tones have been chosen for the planting arrangement as they best complement the silvery-gray of the trough and shells. If you pick your own display, try to stick to one color—a mixture may detract from the decorative impact of the container.

materials & equipment

standard 24 x 10 inch (600 x 250 mm) plain concrete trough

5 large scallop shells

1 quart (1 liter) dark gray undercoat

small jar Japan goldsize and aluminum leaf

paintbrush

two-part epoxy and hardener adhesive

pot shards and 30 quarts (30 liters) potting soil

pot-grown plants in 3 to 4-inch (80 to100-mm) pots, as follows:

5 delphiniums (Delphinium belladonna hybrid 'Wendy')

5 cherry pie heliotropes (Heliotropium peruvianum 'Royal Marine')

5 laurentia axialaris 'Blue Star'

5 Aptenia cordifolia 'Variegata'

metal

Lead is one of the most beautiful metals and patinates naturally outdoors.
Cast iron can look well if left to rust, though it is usually painted; dark
colors tend to work better than light, and the surface must be primed
against corrosion before applying paint. Galvanized tin or wirework is an
attractive outdoor finish that can either be painted or left in its original gray-
ish-silver reflective state. For a touch of glitter add a gold or silver leaf detail.

far left A deep galvanized potato picker painted in dark green high gloss paint makes a good jardinière for larger seasonally-changed plants. Here shown with *Lilium reinesse*—left in their plastic pots so that they can easily be changed at the end of the in season.

center left A tall campagna-shaped cast iron urn. This shape of urn can take a taller mass of planting than the shallower type. Dahlias give a suitable late 19th-century effect from summer through to early autumn.

left A tall galvanized pot is best used with seasonal planting in a raised plastic liner, in this case planted for late spring to early summer with lilies that suit the slender, upright shape of this particular container.

right A 19th-century style wirework stand, very useful for showing a seasonally changing display of plants in terra-cotta pots. Ferns would have been *de rigueur* in the second half of the century; display them with white annuals. Paint wirework a color that will show up against its background— here a dark color to read against a pale blue wall.

above A shallow cast iron urn is filled with coleus, the tender foliage plant loved by the Victorians for its rich, rather artificial-looking variegated colors, reminiscent of the damasks of the period.

left A deep galvanized tub with a basket-work pyramid supports nasturtiums and sweet peas. Create the same effect with a trellis obelisk or cane wigwam used with quick growing climbers like hops, vines, and clematis.

far left Osteospermums in a shallow galvanized tub will have a long summer flowering season. They are now available in a wide color range and with different petal shapes.

wirework basket

This unusual wirework basket is more of an enclosure than a
container; such edgings were used in the early 19th century as a
support and surround for plants. A galvanized iron strip at the bottom
creates a border around a basket-like stand that acts as an attractive
frame for rambling rose bushes. The best roses to use for this
project are low-growing ground cover roses, but you can adapt the
basket to fit any size plant, such as larger shrub roses.

materials & equipment

*1 sheet 48 x 12 inches (1200 x 300 mm) galvanized iron (use a gauge that can
be cut with tin cutters)*

6 galvanized roofing bolts, ½ inch (10 mm) long and ¼ inch (6 mm) wide

72 ft (22 m) of ⅜-inch- (5-mm-) wide galvanized fencing wire

1 piece 21 x 14 x 1 inch (525 x 350 x 25 mm) plywood

tin cutters

jigsaw, hacksaw, and vise or clamps

small pot of gray-blue metal primer

roll of thin galvanized wire

well-rotted manure and rose fertilizer

5 bare-root roses (Rosa 'The Fairy')

galvanized buckets

Hanging galvanized buckets on "S" hooks is an inexpensive and attractive way of displaying plants. A bright and vibrant arrangement such as the one used here adds a splash of color, decoration, and movement to a blank space of wall in a simple setting. Pick similar flowers in sharp colors and bold shapes to contrast with the plain outline and shiny silver-gray surface of the buckets. For immediate results buy pot-grown plants.

materials & equipment

3 galvanized buckets with a 12-inch (300-mm) diameter

3 galvanized angle brackets with 8½-inch- (220-mm-) long tops and 10-inch- (250-mm-) long sides

3 threaded eye bolts with nuts and 3 "S" hooks, 3 inches (80 mm) long

no. 10 plated screws, 2 inches (50 mm) long

pot shards and 15 quarts (15 litres) soil-based potting medium

4 African marigolds (Tagetes erecta)

2 pot marigolds (Calendula officinalis)

2 artemisia 'Powys Castle'

2 single chrysanthemums

2 rudbeckias (R. hirta)

lead-faced trough

The appearance of a lead container can be simulated by fixing sheet lead to a wooden framework. This provides a much cheaper alternative to solid cast lead. Lead patinates to a beautiful silvery-gray color, an effect that is simple and quick to achieve. Take care over size and placement; a window box must sit within the frame and be secured on brackets, and the character and architecture of your building must be considered to ensure that its style is not at odds with that of the trough.

materials & equipment

standard 38 x 10 x 9 inches (950 x 250 x 230 mm) wooden box; or to make

your own cut, in ¾-inch (20-mm) plywood: 2 pieces 38 x 10 inches (950 x 250

mm) front and back; 2 sides, 7½ x 10 inches (190 x 250 mm); 1 base, 38 x 9

inches (950 x 230 mm) and in 1 x 1-inch (25 x 25-mm) softwood: 4 side sup-

ports 10 inches (250 mm) long; 2 base supports 34½ inches (860 mm) long

for softwood molding, cut 2 pieces 11¼ x 1¼ x 1¼ inches (285 x 30 x 30 mm)

and 1 piece 40½ x 1¼ x 1¼ inches (1030 x 30 x 30 mm); for face, 2 sheets gauge

4 lead, 57 x 10 inches (1430 x 250 mm) and 62 x 5 inches (1550 x 130 mm)

no. 8 plated Phillips Screws, 1½ inches (40 mm) long

galvanized roofing nails, 20 mm (¾ in) long

1 quart (1 liter) clear wood preservative and 1 bottle white vinegar

3 each: pink bellflowers (Campanula carpatica), purple nemesias (N.

caerulea) and Persian violets (Exacum affine), 4 osteospermums

(O. 'Whirly Gig'), 5 purple petunias (P. 'Ruby') and 6 senecios (S. cineraria)

wirework hanging basket

A 19th-century wirework basket makes an attractive hanging display. This one is particularly large, making it all the more striking. Anything larger would not be practical because of the weight of the plants and soil. Site it on its own between an upstairs window and a door or place two on either side of a front door.

materials & equipment

24-inch (600-mm) diameter wirework basket

no. 10 Phillips plated screws, 1½ inches (40 mm) long, and wall anchors

galvanized angle bracket with 14-inch (350-mm) top

threaded eye bolt with nuts to fit angle bracket and large "S" hook

peat- or fiber-based lightweight potting medium, and sphagnum moss

pot-grown plants in 3-inch (80-mm) plastic pots as follows:

*10 petunias (*P. surfina*)*

*5 fuchsias (*F. 'Margaret'*)*

*5 pelargoniums (*P. 'Balcon Royale'*)*

*6 petunias (*P. 'Express Ruby'*)*

*6 heliotropes (*Heliotropium peruvianum*)*

*6 tobacco plants (*Nicotiana 'Domino Pink'*)*

painted galvanized washtub

A galvanized tin or enamel bath can be turned into an elegant planter by adding ball feet to give it the look of an early 19th-century jardinière. This planter is good for a large mass of seasonal bedding and looks well on the floor or raised on a low plinth or wall. Paint it to suit the color of your plants and surroundings.

materials & equipment

oval tin tub, 24 inches (600 mm) long and 18 inches (450 mm) wide

1 piece 18 x 14 x ¾ inches (450 x 350 x 20 mm) exterior-grade plywood

4 turned wooden balls with 2½-inch (65-mm) diameter, and 4 separate ⅜-inch (7-mm) dowels, 2 inches (50 mm) long

glue (waterproof PVA)

small jar Japan goldsize

1 packet or twelve 2 x 2-inch (50 x 50-mm) squares gold leaf or Dutch metal

½ quart (½ liter) each of clear wood preservative and dark red undercoat for feet

1 quart (1 liter) flat latex paint

30 quarts (30 liters) potting soil and bag of moss

36 dwarf pink and red tobacco plants (Nicotiana Domino Series)

right A box standard (*Buxus sempervirens*) in a Versailles case creates a smart, well-defined planting. Place cases in pairs to demarcate a front door or garden gate, or to flank the entrance to a formal terrace or garden.

below This twig-work container is a modern variant on 19th-century rustic work. The sculpted character of this planter means that simple shapes and colors work best, allowing the design to be fully appreciated. In this case it has been planted with a box (*Buxus sempervirens*).

below right Evergreen shrubs create a satisfactory dark green mound that suits this tall coopered tub. Custom-made coopered planters tend to be of better proportions than halved barrels. If the steel bands are not galvanized make sure they are painted to reduce rusting.

above A chrysanthemum trained as a standard makes a good formal planting for a Versailles case. These cases need a reasonable bulk of foliage or a precisely clipped head.

right A Victorian shoe-cleaning box makes a good planter. If it is not painted or finished, treat it with wood preservative before planting. Here the box is filled with chrysanthemums. Many carriers or boxes designed for other purposes make good planters or jardinières.

wood

Wood offers the most varied choice of containers, from a formal 17th-century Versailles case to metal-banded coopered tubs. Paint or stain the surface unless it is oak, which will weather to a pleasant silver-gray color.

above A shallow coopered tub is planted with the poached egg plant (*Limnanthes douglasii*), which provides a useful mass of low white-yellow flowers.

left Sedums in a shallow wooden box. The clump-forming perennial *Sedum spectabile* is a very useful container plant, its mass of foliage being as attractive as its compact, yellow-centered flower heads.

below A paneled wooden window box has been planted with variegated ivy and *Capsicum annuum* 'Holiday Time.' Place at ground level on a paved terrace to act as a narrow border.

a rustic window box

The fashion for producing objects that were covered in barked wood originated in the 18th century. This particular design is based on a style developed by the landscape gardener Humphry Repton, who imitated the forms of classical architecture using rustic materials such as barked columns and pine cone festoons. This window box is suited to a rather informal style of planting such as this selection of shade-loving ferns.

materials & equipment

exterior-grade plywood and planed softwood (see step 1, opposite)

1 quart (1 liter) each of clear wood preservative and green wood stain

13 feet (4 m) halved barked poles with 2 to 2½-inch (50 to 65-mm) diameter

3 large and 8 small pine cones

no. 8 plated Phillips screws, 1½ inches (20 mm) long

galvanized roofing nails, 3 inches (80 mm) long

finishing nails, 2 and 2½ inches (50 and 65 mm) long

pot shards and 30 quarts (30 liters) peat-based potting medium

*3 male ferns (*Dryopteris filix-mas*)*

*6 crested female ferns (*Athyrium filix-femina cristatum*)*

9 white impatiens

small bag of sphagnum moss

a Versailles case

A Versailles case is a wooden box that was used at the Palace of
Versailles in the 17th century for growing exotics such as oranges,
lemons, and palms, which could then be easily moved into the
orangery and greenhouses for the winter. The great advantage of
the Versailles case is that it can be unscrewed when the plants need
repotting, or used as a decorative exterior for housing plants in
plastic boxes or pots.

materials & equipment

sawn timber (see step 1, opposite)

*4 finials with ½-inch (10-mm) dowels, or 4 wooden balls or pyramids with
separate ½-inch (10-mm) dowels*

14¾ x 14¾ x ½-inch (375 x 375 x 10-mm) square of exterior-grade plywood

no. 8 screws, 2 inches (50 mm) and 1½ inches (40 mm) long

glue (waterproof PVA)

1 quart (1 liter) wood preservative or oil-based primer

wood stain or flat latex paint

pot shards and 50 quarts (50 liters) moist potting soil

*flowering tea tree (*Leptospermum scoparium*)*

a wood and trellis camouflage box

This container is designed to mask plants in plastic pots for seasonally changing arrangements. There is no base—simply fit it over your potted plants, enclosing the display within a decorated wooden case. A useful disguise for unattractive pots, this box also enables you to mix plant varieties that have different soil and feeding requirements.

materials & equipment

2 pieces 24 x 15 x ¾ inches (600 x 380 x 20 mm) exterior-grade plywood

2 pieces 22½ x 15 x ¾ inches (560 x 380 x 20 mm) exterior-grade plywood

4 pieces 30 x 2 x 2 inches (750 x 50 x 50 mm) planed softwood

44 feet (13,600mm) length of 1 x 1½ inches (25 x 10 mm) planed softwood

1 quart (1 liter) each of clear wood preservative and flat latex paint

2-inch (50-mm) and 1-inch (25-mm) finishing nails

glue (waterproof PVA)

no. 8 Phillips Screws, 2 inches (50 mm) long

16 standard size bricks

4 marguerites (Chrysanthemum frutescens) in 10-inch (250-mm)

diameter plastic pots

trough with trellis screen

This trellis-backed trough is essentially a portable container for tall plants and climbers and can be moved around to rearrange the architectural layout of a garden. This versatile trough acts as both a screen and a planter and is ideal for a balcony or roof garden where it is difficult to support posts.

materials & equipment

lumber (see step 1, opposite)

no. 8 plated Phillips screws, 1½ inches (40 mm), 2½ inches (65 mm), and 4 inches (100 mm) long

finishing nails, 1½ inches (40 mm) long

1 piece 33¾ x 13¾ x ¾ inch (845 x 345 x 20 mm) exterior-grade plywood

45 feet (13.7 m) of 1¼ x ¾ inch (30 x 20 mm) trellis

1 quart (1 liter) wood preservative and ½ gallon (2½ liters) wood stain

pot shards and 50 quarts (50 liters) potting soil

*1 trachelospermum (*T. jasminoides*)*

*2 lesser periwinkles (*Vinca minor*)*

*3 sky-blue lesser periwinkles (*Vinca minor *'Azurea Flore Plena')*

*10 petunias (*P. *'Dark Blue Dwarf')*

planted entrance containers

It is often useful to be able to raise plants high up so that they can be seen from a distance. Use the planters in pairs to simulate gateposts or as part of a screen to mark a division in the garden. These wooden gate piers have been designed as cachepots; the individual plants remain in their plastic pots and can be changed seasonally.

materials & equipment

1 sheet 96 x 48 x ½ inch (2400 x 1200 x 10 mm) exterior-grade plywood

2 squares 11½ x 11½ x ½ inch (290 x 290 x 10 mm) exterior-grade plywod

sawn timber or planed softwood (see steps, opposite)

exterior-grade wood preservative or oil-based primer

½ gallon (2½ liters) flat latex or microporous paint

glue (waterproof PVA)

finishing nails, 2 inches (50 mm) long

galvanized roofing nails, 1½ inches (40 mm) long

no. 8 Phillips Screws, 1¼ inches (30 mm) and 3 inches (75 mm) long

4 hydrangeas (Hydrangea macrophylla)

a wooden obelisk

Trellis obelisks have long been used as a decorative element in the garden. They create an attractive feature on their own, or in pairs can frame a view or emphasize a formal approach to a house. The shape of the obelisk makes it suitable for supporting climbers such as ivy, clematis, honeysuckle, or hops. In this project quick-growing hawthorn has been used; as it spreads, the trellis is used as a clipping guide to create a tall, elegant pyramid shape.

materials & equipment

sawn timber (see steps, opposite)

15 x 15 x ½-inch (380 x 380 x 10-mm) square of exterior-grade plywood

no. 8 screws, 1½ inches (40 mm) and 2 inches (50 mm) long

finishing nails, 1½ inches (40 mm) long

1 quart (1 liter) clear wood preservative or oil-based primer

1 quart (1 liter) wood stain

pot shards and 50 quarts (50 litres) potting soil

*4 bare-root hawthorns (*Crataegus monogyna*)*

primula theater

This design for a primula theater is for a scaled-down version of an early 19th-century type of shaded staging, made to show off the best examples in a collection and to protect the flowers from sun and rain. It will hold up to fifteen 4-inch (100-mm) pots comfortably; terra-cotta pots look best. Paint or stain the theater dark blue, dark green, gray, or black to form a good background for the rich and varied colors of the primulas.

materials and equipment

planed softwood or sawn timber (see steps, opposite)

shuttering or other exterior-grade plywood (see steps, opposite)

1 quart (1 liter) wood preservative or oil-based primer

galvanized nails and finishing nails

glue (waterproof PVA)

microporous paint or wood stain

13 terra-cotta pots with 4-inch (100-mm) diameters

Primula vulgaris

Primula denticulata

Primula veris

Primula *Gold Lace Group*

plant directory

Key

Zones are based on the average annual minimum temperature for each zone; the smaller number indicates the northernmost zone it can survive in; the higher number, the southernmost zone the plant will tolerate.

H   Height   S   Spread
Z   Zone

Z 1: below -50°F (-45°C)   Z 7: 0-10°F (-18 to -12°C)
Z 2: -50 to -40°F (-45 to -40°C) Z 8: 10-20°F (-12 to -7°C)
Z 3: -40 to -30°F (-40 to -34°C) Z 9: 20-30°F (-7 to -1°C)
Z 4: -30 to -20°F (-34 to -29°C) Z 10: 30-40°F (-1 to 4°C)
Z 5: -20 to -10°F (-29 to -23°C) Z 11: above 40°F (4°C)
Z 6: -10 to 0°F (-23 to -18°C)

Acanthus mollis (Bear's breeches)
H: 3-4ft (90-120 cm); S: 4 ft (120 cm); Z: 8-10
Herbaceous perennial with large, beautifully shaped leaves, much used in classical ornamentation. White or pink flowers come in July to August on 18-inch (45-cm) long spikes. Prefers full sun.

Agapanthus africanus **'Headbourne Hybrids'**
H: 3 ft (1 m); S: 20 in (50 cm); Z: 7-10
Late summer flowering perennial. Deep blue-violet bell-shaped flowers and long evergreen leaves. Plant in well-drained soil in sun or light shade. Cover in winter or keep in a greenhouse.

Ageratum houstonianum **'Blue Danube'**
H and S: 6 in (15 cm)
Summer flowering annual with blue, purple, and pink heart-shaped flowers. Sow in a warm greenhouse and plant out late.

Anthemis nobile **'Treneague'** (Lawn chamomile)
H: 1 in (2.5 cm); S: 18 in (45 cm); Z: 4-8
Moss-like carpet of non-flowering grass with aromatic leaves; plant in a well drained area.

Aptenia cordifolia **'Variegata'**
H: 2 in (5 cm); S: indefinite; Z: 4-8
Low-growing perennial succulent. Cream-edged leaves and daisy-like blue and pink flowers in summer. Prefers well-drained soil.

Artemesia **'Powys Castle'**
H: 24-36 in (60-90 cm); S: 4 ft (1.2 m); Z: 6-9
Perennial dwarf, non-flowering silver-leaved variety, likes well-drained compost and full sun. Clip back in spring to keep compact.

Aster (Michaelmas daisy)
A genus of perennials and deciduous or evergreen shrubs with daisy-like flowers. Likes well-drained soil and a sunny aspect.
A. novae-belgii **'Audrey'**
H and S: 12 in (30 cm); Z: 4-8
Pale blue, semi-double pointed flowers.
A. novae-belgii **'Snowsprite'**
H and S: 12 in (30 cm); Z: 4-8
Produces white slender-pointed flowers in autumn. Plant in autumn or spring.

Athyrium filix-femina cristatum (Crested female fern)
H and S: 3 ft (90 cm); Z: 4-8
Fern with tall lacy fresh green crested fronds. Water freely March to October. Remove dead foliage in spring.

Aucuba japonica 'Crotonifolia'
H: 6-9 ft (1.8-2.7 m); Z: 7-9
Evergreen shrub best grown in shade. The
speckled yellow and green leaves withstand
urban pollution. 'Borealis' is a dwarf green
variety.

Aurinia saxatalis (syn. *Alyssum saxatile*)
H: 9 in (23 cm); S: 12 in (30 cm); Z: 3-7
Shrub with gray foliage and light yellow
clusters of flowers. Likes full sun. Cut back
after flowering.

Buxus sempervirens (Common box)
H: up to 15 ft (4.5 m); Z: 5-8
Medium sized evergreen shrub or small tree
that thrives in sun or shade. Usually used for
dwarf hedges or for topiary. Produces
luxurious masses of small dark evergreen
leaves. Trim after growth in summer to
maintain a uniform shape. (See below.)

Calendula officinalis (Pot marigold)
H and S: 20-28 in (50-70 cm)
Annual with yellow to orange flowers in
summer and autumn. Likes well-drained soil
and full sun. Self-seeds.

Camellia japonica (Common camellia)
H: up to 30 ft (9 m); Z: 7-9
Evergreen lime-hating shrub or small tree
with large flowers in varying colors in early
spring. Will grow up to 6 ft (1.8 m) in a large
tub. Acid to neutral peaty soil works best,
prefers a light shaded position. 'Mathotiana
Alba' is a good white double variety.

Campanula carpatica (Bell flower)
H: 3-4 in (8-10 cm); S: 12 in (30 cm); Z: 3-8
Rock perennial with blue, mauve, or
lavender-blue flowers, either solitary or
several to a stem. Flowers freely in summer in
an open or semi-shaded position and well-
drained soil.

Citrus limon 'Meyer'
H: 18-24 in (45-60 cm) ; S: 18-20 in
(45-50 cm); Z: 9-10
Evergreen medium to large shrub with large
bright green leaves and heavily scented white
flowers in spring and summer followed by
large lemons; flowers and fruits together.
Overwinter in a greenhouse or conservatory,
but may be put outside after frosts in a
sheltered sunny place. Keep well watered in
summer months.

Chaenomeles japonica 'Alba'
H: 3-12 ft (1-3.7 m); Z: 4-8
Deciduous shrub with early spring flowers—
these have white flowers. This plant will
happily grow in a shaded environment. It is a
good idea to cut back immediately after
flowering in order to keep the shape
compact.

Chrysanthemum frutescens, syn. *Argyranthemum
frutescens* (Marguerites)
H and S: 3 ft (1 m); Z: 8-10
Shrubby perennial with grayish foliage and
white or yellow daisy-like flowers with yellow
centers. Flowers over a long summer period
if deadheaded. Train as a standard or tight
ball by pinching out the foliage ends. Do not
put out until the end of May. (See below.)

Convolvulus sabatius (syn. *C. mauritanicus*)
H: 6-8 in (15-20 cm); S: 12 in (30 cm); Z: 8-10
Rock trailing perennial, blue-mauve flowers.

Coreopsis tincturia (Tickseed)
H: 2-3 ft (60-90 cm); S: 8 in (20 cm)
Annual with yellow to crimson brown-edged
flowers in summer. Also colored hybrids.

Cordyline indivisa (syn. *Dracaena indivisa*)
H: 10 ft (3 m); S: 6 ft (2 m); Z: 8-10
Evergreen tree or shrub with long spiky
leaves—gray with red or yellow stripe.

Crataegus monogyna (Common hawthorn)
H: up to 20 ft (6 m); Z: 4-7
Quick growing deciduous small tree. White flowers and red fruit and autumn foliage. Excellent for quick topiary; clip throughout the growing season.

Cyclamen
A genus of tuberous perennials with pendulous flowers and five reflexed petals. Likes a sunny aspect and well-drained soil.
C. cilicium
H: 4 in (10 cm); S: 2-4 in (5-10 cm); Z: 6-9
Roundish leaves with silvery markings and pale pink flowers in autumn.
C. hederifolium
H: 4 in (10 cm); S: 2-4 in (5-10 cm); Z: 5-9
Ivy-shaped leaves with scented pink flowers in autumn, from September to October.

Daphne odora '**Aureomarginata**'
H and S: 5 ft (1.5 m); Z: 4-7
Dwarf evergreen spreading shrub. Narrow leaves have a yellow margin and the white flowers are very fragrant. Place in a sunny sheltered position.

Delphinium Belladonna '**Wendy**'
H: 24 in (60 cm); S: 8 in (20 cm); Z: 5-9
Perennial with gentian blue flowers in summer. Also available in pale blue, white, and pink. (See below.)

Dryopteris filix-mas (Male fern)
H and S: 16 in (40 cm); Z: 4-9
Deciduous or semi-evergreen bright green fern. Needs shade and humus-rich soil. Keep moist.

Exacum affine (Persian violet)
H: 6 in (15 cm)
Annual with bluish lilac fragrant flowers in June to October. Water freely and overwinter indoors.

Festuca glauca (Blue fescue)
H and S: 23 cm (9 in); Z: 4-8
Perennial thin-leaved grass forms bright blue to gray dense tufts. At its best in the sun from spring to midsummer.

Fuchsia
Genus of deciduous shrubs with pendulous bell-shaped flowers. Plant in a sunny place and cover roots with mulch.
F. '**Margaret**'
H: 3 ft (1 m); S: 2½ ft (75 cm); Z: 9-10
Vigorous shrub. Crimson and violet purple semi-double flowers.
F. x *speciosa* '**La Bianca**'
H and S: 2 ft (60 cm); Z: 9-10
Hybrid shrub. Flowers are pink. Overwinter in a cool greenhouse, put out in May. Train as a half or full standard. (See below.)

Gazania '**Orange Beauty**'
H and S: 12 in (30 cm); Z: 5-9
Perennial that displays brilliant orange flowers from late June and has silver-gray foliage. Plant in late May in light sandy soil in the sun. Protect from frost. A variety of colors is available.

Hebe pinguifolia '**Pagei**'
H: 6-12 in (15-30 cm); S: 2-3 ft (60-100 cm); Z: 7-9. Dwarf evergreen gray-leaved shrub. Forms very satisfactory gray foliage mounds. White flowers in late spring.

Hedera (Ivy)
A genus of evergreen woody-stemmed, trailing perennials with green or variegated lobed leaves. Prefers well-drained soil.
H. helix (Common English ivy)
H and S: up to 10 ft (3 m); Z: 6-9
Climbing or trailing evergreen, also 'self branching.' Can be trained over frames. Other varieties include *H. helix* 'Glacier,' *H. helix* 'Autropureum,' and *H. helix* 'Adam.'

H. helix **'Erecta'** (Upright ivy)
H: 30 ft (10 m); S: 15 ft (5 m); Z: 6-9
Upright form of *Hedera helix*. Useful clipped in window boxes as an alternative to box or as a year round support structure for seasonal planting.

Helianthus **'Loddon Gold'** (Sunflower)
H: 4-5 ft (1.2-1.5 m)
Annual with double golden yellow flowers in July to September. Needs sun. (See below.)

Heliotropium peruvianum **'Royal Marine'** (Heliotrope, Cherry Pie)
H: 15-36 in (38-90 cm); S: 12-15 in (30-38 cm); Z: 9-10
This purplish green-leaved perennial has heavily scented deep violet blue flowers. Needs to be planted in a sunny position in early June. Overwinter in a cool greenhouse or conservatory. Can be trained as a standard on a cane. (See below.)

Holcus mollis **'Albovariegatus'** (Creeping soft-grass)
H: 12-18 in (30-45 cm); S: indefinite; Z: 4-9
Evergreen, spreading perennial grass with white-and-green varigated foliage. In summer it carries purplish-white flower spikes.

Hosta
A genus of herbaceous perennials grown for abundant foliage ranging from blues to silver-green and golden colors. Will tolerate shade and prefers damp soil.
H. fortunei **var.** *aureamarginata*
H: 2 ft (60 cm); Z: 3-9
Leaves are edged in yellow and late spring flowers are lilac.
H. sieboldiana **var.** *elegans*
H: 2-3 ft (60-90 cm); Z: 3-9
Bold blue-green foliage and violet flowers in early summer.

Hyacinthus orientalis **'Delft Blue'**
H: 10 in (25 cm); S: 6 in (15 cm); Z: 4-8
Pale blue heavily scented flowers produced from a bulb in April. Plant from mid-September. Water well when growing. Other colors and dwarf varieties available.

Hydrangea macrophylla **'Blue Wave'** (Lace cap hydrangea)
H: up to 6 ft (1.8 m); Z: 6-9
Deciduous shrub, has dense heads of variable blue flowers in summer. In alkaline soils flowers change to pink. Add aluminum sul-phate to change back to blue. (See below.)

Ilex (Holly)
Evergreen deciduous trees or shrubs with glossy green foliage and berries. Tolerates sun and shade. Prefers to be planted in well-drained soil.
I. x *meserveae* **'Blue Prince'**
H: up to 10 ft (3 m); Z: 7-9
Vigorous growth of dark blue-green foliage.
I. aquifolium **'Silver Queen'**
H: 20 ft (5 m); S: 12 ft (4 m); Z: 7-9
Variegated leaves of green mottled gray with white margins and reddish stems and no berries. Often grown as a standard. Clips well into dense formal shape. Is paradoxically a male plant.

I. crenata
H: 15 ft (5 m); S: 10 ft (3 m); Z: 6-8
Tiny box-like dark green leaves. Keeps a
compact shape when pruned.

Impatiens balsamina (Busy Lizzy)
H: 9 in (23 cm); Z: 5-9
Annuals available in wide range of colors
with both double and single flowers. Place in
a sheltered sunny position in rich moist
compost.

Laurentia axialaris 'Blue Star'
H: 6 in (15 cm)
Small growing annual related to the lobelia.
Pale blue mauve flowers from June onward
and light green foliage. Put in full sun and
use well-drained soil.

Leptospermum scoparium (Tea tree)
H: up to 10 ft (3 m); Z: 9-10
Evergreen shrub with dark grayish green
leaves and small pink flowers that begin in
early summer and continue over a long
period. Overwinter in a cool greenhouse.
Good flowering topiary subject; clip to retain
dense foliage head. (See below.)

Lilium reinesse
H: 12 in (30 cm); Z: 4-9
Bulb produces pale yellow flowers in
summer. Likes well-drained soil. Deadhead
and keep out of direct sun.

Linaria cymbalaria (Ivy-leaved toadflax)
H: 4-6 in (10-15 cm); Z: 4-8
Trailing perennial with lilac flowers in summer. Good in hanging baskets. Water freely
in summer and keep virtually dry in winter.

Lobelia erinus 'Pendula Blue Cascade'
H: 4-8 in (10-20 cm); S: 4-6 in (10-15 cm)
Trailing annual. Light blue flowers in
summer, good in hanging baskets.

Morus alba 'Pendula' (Weeping Mulberry)
H: 6-8 ft (1.8-2.5 m); Z: 4-10
Deciduous tree with attractive weeping
foliage and mulberry fruit. Protect from
strong winds. Prune in February, thinning
overcrowded branches. Plant from October
to March.

Myosotis alpestris (Forget-me-not)
H and S: 6-9 in (15-23 cm)
Biennial or perennial. Pot up early autumn.
Pale blue flowers appear in mid-spring to
early summer. A beautiful feathery underplanting for tulips. Available in white and
various dark blues. (See below.)

Nemesia caerulea
H: 10 in (25 cm)
Annual, plant out in June in sun. Propagate
by seed sown in March.

Nicotiana (Tobacco plant)
Genus of perennials treated as annuals with
tubular scented flowers. Plant in well-drained
soil for summer flowering.
N. alata 'Lime Green'
H: 2 ft (60 cm); S: 1 ft (30 cm)
Lime-green flower; sow seed in warm green-
house February to March. Keep well watered.
Available in dwarf forms. (See below.)

N. 'Domino Pink'
H and S: 18 in (30 cm)
Bushy plants characterized by bright
magenta pink flowers. Other colors
available in Domino Series. (See below.)

Osteospermum
Genus of evergreen semi-woody perennials.
Suits a sunny aspect and well-drained soil.
Produces sprawling daisy-like flowers in
summer to early autumn.
O. 'Buttermilk'
H: 2 ft (60 cm); S: 1 ft (30 cm); Z: 6-9
Large butter-yellow daisy-like flowers with
dark eyes.
O. 'Whirly Gig'
H: 2 ft (60 cm); S: 12-18 in (30-45 cm); Z: 6-9
White paddle-shaped petals. (See below.)

Pelargonium 'Balcon Royale'
Trails: 12-24 in (30-60 cm)
Perennial grown as annual. Trailing ivy-
leaved pelargonium with bluish red flowers
in mid-spring to mid-autumn. Overwinter
indoors and display in dry sunny conditions.
Pelargonium 'Friesdorf'
H: 10 in (25 cm); S: 6 in (15 cm)
A zonal evergreen perennial. Characterized
by dark green foliage and scarlet-orange
flowers with thin petals.

Petunia
A genus of annuals characterized by showy
flowers in a variety of colors, either
Grandiflora or Multiflora. They need plenty
of sun and well-drained soil.

P. surfina
H: 9-12 in (23-30 cm)
Numerous named hybrids are also available.
Plant out late May to June and deadhead to
make the most of the long flowering season.
P. 'Dark Blue Dwarf'
H: 8 in (20 cm)
Rich blue flowers, well suited to small pots.
P. 'Express Ruby'
H: 9-12 in (23-30 cm)
Large purple flowers with dark throats.

Phlox drummondii
H: 6-12 in (15-30 cm); S: 4 in (10 cm)
Annual, available in pink, mauve and red.
Plant out late May to June. Prefers moist
sunny or partially shaded conditions.

Phyllitis scolopendrium (syn. *Asplenium
scolopendrium*)
H: 12-18 in (30-45 cm); S: 18 in (45 cm);
Z: 5-9. Fern with light green elegantly curved
fronds. Pot February to March. Water freely
March to October. Overwinter in a greenhouse or conservatory. Prefers shade.

Pittosporum tenuifolium 'Purpureum'
H: 6 ft (1.8 m); S: 13 ft (4 m); Z: 8-10
Evergreen large shrub or small tree. Pale
green leaves gradually change to deep
bronze purple. Honey-scented flowers in
spring. Can be cut back.

Polygala myrtifolia
H and S: 5 ft (1.5 m)
Flowering evergreen shrub with pale green
leaves and bright purple pea flowers. Overwinter in a greenhouse or conservatory.

Primula (Primrose)

A genus of annuals, biennials and perennials that generally enjoy sunny positions and thrive best in well-drained soil. Characterized by basal leaves and primrose-shaped flowers.

P. vulgaris

H: 6 in (15 cm); S: 10 in (25 cm); Z: 5-8

Perennial with short thick leaves and pale yellow flowers with darker centers in late winter and spring. Look good as a single plant or in shallow containers in clumps.

P. denticulata

H: 12-18 in (30-45 cm); Z: 4-8

Perennial that comes in shades of mauve or white with round heads on long stems in spring and has long toothed leaves. Works well as a single specimen.

P. veris (Cowslip)

H and S: 6-8 in (15-20 cm); Z: 5-8

Native perennial with rounded long leaves and small, deep yellow flowers in long-stalked clusters in spring.

P. polyanthus Gold Lace Group (Gold laced polyanthus)

H: 6-8 in (15-20 cm); Z: 3-8

Spring flowering perennial with round heads in a variety of gold edged colors. A large number of named varieties exist, hybridized since the mid-18th century.

Prunus lusitanica (Portugal laurel)

H and S: 20 ft (6 m); Z: 7-10

Evergreen shrub or small tree with ovate dark green glossy leaves and small white hawthorn-scented flowers in June. Small red fruits turning to dark purple in autumn. A good subject for mop-head standards. Tolerates shade.

Pyracantha coccinea

H and S: 12 ft (4 m); Z: 6-9

Evergreen shrub, densely branched with white flowers in large clusters in summer followed by red or orange-red berries in large bunches in autumn to winter. Prune to keep a compact shape; can be espaliered or pruned. Tolerant of all exposures, pollution and shade.

Rhododendron

H: 6-8 ft (2-2.5 m); Z: 5-8

Mainly evergreen shrubs with attractive glossy foliage. Spring to summer flowering in a range of colors. Deadhead after flowering. Prune in April to keep in shape. Good hybrids for containers are: 'Cunningham's White' (white), 'Cynthia' (rose-crimson), 'Doncaster' (crimson-scarlet).

Rosa (Rose)

A genus of deciduous or semi-evergreen shrubs and scrambling climbers. Grown for flowers that are often fragrant, with leaves that have five to seven oval leaflets. The stems are usually thorny or with prickles. Plant in well-drained soil.

R. 'Sanders' White Rambler'

H: 4-5 ft (1.2-1.5 m); Z: 4-9

Small scented white flowers in cascading clusters. Available as a container-grown weeping standard. (See below.)

R. 'The Fairy'

H: 2 ft (60 cm); S: 4 ft (120 cm); Z: 4-9

Polyantha spreading rose good for shallow containers. Produces clusters of beadlike buds that open to globular pink flowers throughout the summer. Shade tolerant. Available as container-grown standard and half-standard. (See below.)

R. 'White pet'

H: 2 ft (60 cm); Z: 4-9

A 19th-century Polyantha short-growing rose producing huge trusses of pure white pompom-like blooms throughout summer. This rose will tolerate a shaded position. Available as a container-grown standard and half-standard.

R. Nozomi
H: 2 ft (60 cm); Z: 5-9
Ground cover rose with small pearly pink to white flowers produced in abundance. Ideal for hanging over the edge of containers.

Rudbeckia hirta (Cone flower)
H: 2-3 ft (60-90 cm); Z: 4-8
Golden-yellow flowers with dark brown center and long oblong leaves. Plant this flower in a sunny position and make sure you water regularly.

Salvia farinacea 'Rhea'
H: 3 ft (1 m); S: 1 ft (30 cm); Z: 9-10
A perennial with lance-shaped mid-green leaves and violet to blue flowers, from tubular spikes. Prefers well-drained soil and a sunny position.

Sempervivum tectorum (Houseleek)
H and S: 12 in (30 cm); Z: 3-8
Perennial succulent. Forms dense green mound of foliage suitable for a dry sunny position and will survive with virtually no soil and very little water. Good cascading display that works well in architectural designs in urns. (See below.)

Senecio cineraria (syn. *Cineraria maritima*)
(Sea ragwort)
H and S: 1 ft (30 cm); Z: 8-10
Summer-flowering perennial. Has deeply cut gray leaves and yellow flowers midsummer to autumn. 'Silver Dust' is a good non-flowering cultivar.

Tagetes erecta (African marigold)
H: 1-3 ft (30-100 cm)
Annual with single yellow or orange daisy-like flowers that have a long flowering throughout the summer. Plant out in May in a sunny position, use well-drained soil, and water regularly.

Tilia x **europea** (Lime)
H: up to 100 ft (31 m); Z: 4-7
Deciduous tree with yellowish-white fragrant flowers and broadly ovate leaves. Easy to train in containers and can be pleached, pollarded, and generally kept in shape by hard pruning in mid- to late summer. If planting a bare-rooted lime, plant between mid-autumn and spring.

Tilia platyphyllos 'Rubra' (Red-twigged lime)
H: up to 100 ft (31 m); Z: 4-7
Deciduous tree. Young shoots are bright brownish-red and make a particularly effective display in winter.

Trachelospermum jasminoides
H and S: up to 21 ft (6.5 m); Z: 9-10
Slow-growing climbing shrub with narrowly oval dark, shiny green leaves and very fragrant white flowers over a very long period from late spring to autumn. Likes sun and moist soil. Overwinter indoors. Can be trained. (See below.)

Verbena tenera (Italian verbena)
H: 6-18 in (15-45 cm); S: 1 ft (30 cm); Z: 7-9
Summer flowering trailing perennial with blue or violet fragrant flowers. Also *Verbena tenuisecta* f. *alba* in white. Plant in well-drained soil and sun.

Vinca minor (Lesser periwinkle)
H: 6 in (15 cm); S: 5 ft (1.5 m); Z: 7-9
Evergreen trailing shrub with blue to purple small white-centered flowers. *Vinca minor* 'Alba Variegata' produces white flowers. Likes semi-shade and moist soil.
Vinca minor 'Azurea Flore Plena'
H: 6 in (15 cm); S: 5 ft (1.5 m); Z: 7-9
Evergreen trailing shrub. Bright sky-blue flowers on short flowering shoots in spring or summer. Leaves form a dense dark green mat. Best in sun and moist soil.

care and maintenance

BASIC EQUIPMENT

For the Gardener
Container gardening requires only a handful
of tools, and the projects in this book can be
undertaken with just the bare essentials. Use
a wheelbarrow for fetching and moving pots
and mixing compost and a garden cart for
transporting larger containers and general
gardening equipment. A stout cloth or
collecting cloth with handles saves mess
when potting, and can be used to remove
debris. Indispensable hand tools include an
old kitchen knife for weeding pots, a hand
fork and trowel, a dibber to make holes for
seeds or young plants, secateurs, sharp scis-
sors, shears, and a pruning saw. Old garden
tools are often much nicer than new ones;
buy them inexpensively at second hand deal-
ers. Failing that, it is worth investing in some
stainless steel tools, which are easy to keep
clean and wear well. For watering and spray-
ing you need a watering can and a hose. Use
a handheld spray for applying foliar feed and
insecticide and a measuring jug for mixing
them. Gardening can be a grubby business
and wearing on the hands. You can use
special tough gardening gloves to protect
your hands.

For the Woodworker
There are no complicated procedures, joints,
or fixings in the construction projects in this
book. If you can cut a piece of wood and
screw separate pieces together you will be
able to cope. When buying and cutting wood
make sure you follow the measurements
specifed in the projects. Use a handsaw for
cutting timber and plywood to size. A work
bench or pair of sawhorses help when cutting, though a stout table will do. An electric
jigsaw is quick and easy, particularly for
curved cuts, but a coping saw will do. When
choosing a hammer, the claw hammer is the
most versatile type; it has one end for driving
in nails and a curved claw for removing
them, although a pair of pincers are better
for this task. For drilling holes use a metal
brace with appropriate bits or the faster
hand-held electric drill. Most structures are
secured with screws. A no. 2 screwdriver used
with Phillips Screws is standard for these projects. When starting screws use an awl to
make a pilot hole; this marks the position
clearly and prevents the screw driver from
slipping and damaging the surface of the
wood. Other useful items include a pair of
clamps to keep work steady or hold pieces
together and a smoothing plane.

For Painting
Ordinary household paintbrushes are
standard for most of the paintwork, though
for decorative details an artist's brush is more
accurate. Before you begin to paint ensure
that your surface is smooth and clean; a soft-
bristled dusting brush works best. Use paint
thinner to clean the brushes. Other general
equipment includes protective plastic sheets
or paper, plenty of old rags, and exterior-
grade wood filler—use to fill cracks and
indents and smooth with sandpaper.

For Metal Projects
The metal constructions are relatively simple and need only a few special items of equipment. For lead facings and trimmings you need a pair of tin cutters for cutting. It is also a good idea to have a pair of protective gloves when handling lead. For cutting thicker metals a hacksaw is the best instrument. When shaping metal use a vise on a bench together with a mallet to help bend strips. For gilding a range of metal and transfer leaves is available.

WOODWORKING TECHNIQUES

Glues and Fixings
The best adhesive for these constructions is exterior-grade PVA (polyvinyl acetate) glue. Before gluing always make sure surfaces are dust- and grease-free. Let adhesive dry overnight to achieve its full strength. Phillips Screws are the easiest to fix, especially with an electric screwdriver. Usually plated to protect them from rust, they come in a variety of sizes and types. When screwing wood together, pre-drill one piece to fit the screw diameter and pilot drill the other. If you are using an electric screwdriver in softwood a pilot hole may not be necessary. When possible use galvanized finishing nails and galvanized nails to protect against rust. Finishing nails are often used with glue to reinforce a joint. For a neat finish, punch your nail below the surface and fill in the holes with a special wood filler.

Lumber
Softwood is generally specified in the projects, as it is cheap and easy to work. Treat softwood with a clear exterior-grade wood preservative for use outside; this must be applied before any other finish.
Lumber is available in sawn (rough) or planed (smooth) finishes. You should indicate to your lumber merchant which type you want, as it makes a difference to the dimensions. The important thing to note about these two finishes is that the sizes specified for each are the same but the end result is different; for instance a 2 x 1-inch (50 x 25-mm) piece of sawn is the size you actually get, whereas in planed it is only the size the timber starts off before it is planed. The final width and depth of planed timber is about ⅛ to ³⁄₁₆ inches (3 to 5 mm) smaller than the quoted size. A sawn finish is generally better if you are using a decorative stain, because the stain will soak in more easily. Planed finish is better for a painted finish and is really essential if you are using a gloss paint.

Plywood
Plywood is available in a range of thicknesses from ⅛ inch (3 mm) to 1³⁄₁₆ inch (30 mm). The cheapest exterior-grade plywood you can buy is shuttering ply which is suitable for all the projects in the book. More expensive plywoods are available, but these tend to be high quality structural wood, only worth using with hardwood.

Hardwood
Oak and teak are the best hardwoods for using outside, though they are expensive and harder to work. It is better to use a stained finish on them since it is difficult to make paint stay on in the long run.

PAINTS AND STAINS

Preservatives
Treat unpreserved wood with anti-rot, anti-woodworm and fungicide; clear wood preservatives are available for this purpose. These are toxic to plants, so must be applied well in advance of planting. Some preservatives are available specifically for horticultural work, but are often tinted, which can affect the color of a stain applied on top.

Stains
Some stains contain preservative, others are only water-repellent. Stains tend to look better in muted colors and are affected by the color of the wood to which you are applying them; they work most effectively on a sawn lumber finish.

Paint
A wide range of paint types is available for exterior use on wood. They include: oil-based gloss, micro-porous exterior paint, and ordinary exterior latex, which is long lasting. Oil undercoat used on its own is good for a very flat finish. Ordinary water-based paint is effective on terra-cotta, as is oil-bound or water-bound distemper; use watered down to achieve a "distressed" look. Concrete also takes latex paint or special exterior-grade masonry paint. For metal use a gloss paint or a proprietary metal paint.

CHOOSING CONTAINERS

There are two ways of looking at container gardening: either start with the plants you want and find containers suited to the character and habit of the plant, or start with the containers and devise planting plans to suit them. I favor the second approach, since it is the containers that will have the year-round effect and will have to fit in with the character and scale of the setting.

Choosing the Scale

Look at the setting and where you need plant interest. The container would need to be quite bold and simple in outline to show up at a distance. The height of the planting must also be decided in relation to the rest of the garden; generally the taller the planting the larger the container. Elaborate detail is best in a foreground position, where it can be seen clearly. The same applies to planting: complex plans using delicate plants are best seen close up, where their detail can be fully appreciated.

Choosing a Material and Color

The color of your material should harmonize with the house and the rest of the garden as well as with the intended planting plan. In general, materials that weather and patinate are more appealing; hand-thrown terra-cotta patinates the quickest. Lead, stone, and cast stone also patinate with age, and the process can be speeded up by applying vinegar in the case of lead, and yogurt, milk, or liquid manure in the case of stone and cast stone. A useful trick to age a pot is to place it under the drip of trees. Cast iron and wood both need to be painted or stained to preserve them. Use a faded blue-gray-green, referred to as "Versailles blue," a color often seen on the shutters of old houses in Italy and France.

LOOKING AFTER CONTAINERS

Containers need to be scrupulously cleaned and scrubbed before planting, especially if they have been used before; scrub them well on the inside with clean water, but try to preserve the patina on the outside. Some containers are best used with plastic liners—this is particularly important with seasonally changing designs. Plastic liners are particularly useful for large Versailles cases and urns. Check that your terra-cotta is frost proof if

you are going to leave it outside all year round. In winter even hardy plants in pots will need their roots protected against severe frost—wrap the pot with burlap, straw, or bubble wrap (see below).

Where plants are in liners pack straw between the plastic pot and container for protection. In early autumn or spring examine the condition of your containers and repaint them if necessary.

PLANTING MEDIUM

Different plants require different soils. In general all containers need good drainage. See that there are sufficient holes to let out excess moisture, and put in a thin layer of pot shards or gravel in the base of pots to help drainage. For semi-permanent plantings use an aerated nutritious potting soil, and for short-term schemes, a soilless multipurpose medium. Some plants have specific requirements, for instance special composts are available for bulbs, and very gritty free-draining soil-based composts are recommended for some alpine and rock plants. Note whether your plant needs a fast or slow growing medium. Peat-based mixtures are good for containers, as they are light, but they also have a tendency to dry out and so are unsuitable for plants that are difficult to water. Soil-based media are a more stable alternative, but carry more weight. Also available are bark, coir, and wood fiber mixtures that work well in containers.

POTTING PLANTS

The size of the container should relate visually to the size of the planting and should be large enough to contain the root ball and sustain growth. Some plants do not like to be constantly repotted and do not mind being rootbound, whereas others need to be regularly repotted as they grow. Most seasonal plantings, if properly fed and watered, can stand being in a confined pot. For a shrub or tree, start off with a large container that will support its growth for a number of years before the inevitable repotting. Some Versailles cases are specifically designed for ease of repotting; the sides let down for easy removal of the root ball. One might consider such a design for large plants such as orange and lemon trees, camellias, and greenhouse exotics. When potting up a multiple seasonal planting it is sometimes necessary to cram the de-potted root balls in to create the desired effect—one would not consider this for permanent plantings, but in this case, as long as the roots have space to develop downward the plants will survive. For permanent plantings be more careful with root ball placement. Place single specimens centrally in the pot and firm down. Also make sure that the finished soil surface is at least 1 inches (25 mm) below the top edge of the container so that there is space for a water reservoir. With standards, choose a specimen with an upright and secure stem (stake if necessary) as it is much more difficult to correct this later. Climbing plants can have supports fixed in the soil or to the container. There are a wide range of stakes, metal shapes, and trellis obelisks available that you can construct yourself or buy ready-made.

FEEDING AND WATERING

In summer, watering is the key to good container gardening. Small pots, particularly terra-cotta, dry out very quickly and in hot weather will need watering twice a day in early morning and evening to avoid sunburn to wet leaves. Water larger pots only once a day. Always soak the plant thoroughly by filling the reservoir at the top up to the brim. If you are using a hose, use one with a sprinkler nozzle so that the water pressure does not wash away any compost. Reduce watering as the growing season subsides, and in winter most plants only need to be kept from drying out, so check every few days to make sure they are still moist. In some cases plants that are dormant in winter prefer the soil to be almost dry—check individual plants for special needs. A useful way to conserve moisture is to place a layer of mulch over the soil.

There are various methods for feeding container-grown plants. Slow-release granules are good for long-term plantings—sprinkle them onto the surface of the soil and rake them in. Other chemical fertilizers can be mixed into the soil when planting. Liquid fertilizers are diluted in water and used as part of the watering regime. Foliar feeds are sprayed on for instant effect, and organic material can be used as a top dressing. Use homemade compost, well-rotted manure, or blood and bone, applied during the growing season. When planting always follow the specific feed requirements, as some plants like a relatively impoverished soil and do not respond well to overfeeding.

PESTS AND DISEASES

Plants that are stressed by poor watering and feeding are more vulnerable to attack, so the surest way to prevent the invasion of pests and diseases is to take the best care possible of your plants and containers; cleanliness of pots and tools helps keep bacterial diseases at bay, as does keeping a regular eye on their health. Plants are subject to three disease groups: bacterial, fungal, and viral. The last of these is untreatable—destruction of the plant is the only remedy. Below is a typical example of bacterial leaf spot (left) and powdery mildew (right).

There are many different chemicals and organics that can be applied to your plants to rid them of pests and diseases. To find out which ones are most suited to your plants, and also what is available in your area, visit your local garden center. For information about insect and pest control you can try calling the National Pesticide Telecommunications Network at 800-858-7378. Be careful when storing sprays and chemicals, keep them away from children and pets, and wear gloves and a mask as directed.

useful addresses

**NURSERIES AND PLANT
SPECIALISTS**

Bluestone Perennials
7211 Middle Ridge Road
Madison, Ohio
(800) 852-5243
www.bluestoneperennials.com

W. Atlee Burpee Seed Co.
300 Park Avenue
Warminster, PA 18974
(800) 888-1447
www.burpee.com

Carroll Gardens
444 East Main Street
Westminster, MD 21157
(800) 638-6334
(410) 848-5422
www.carrollgardens.com

Dutch Gardens
725 Vassar Avenue
Lakewood, NJ 08701
(800) 818-3861
(732) 780-2713
www.dutchgardens.com

Gurney's Seed & Nursery Co.
110 Capitol Street
Yankton, SD 57079
(800) 824-6400
www.gurneys.com

**Hastings Nature
& Garden Center**
3920 Peachtree Road NE
Atlanta, GA 30319
(404) 869-7447

Jackson & Perkins Co.
One Rose Lane
Medford, OR 97501
(800) 872-7673
(541) 864-2388
www.jacksonandperkins.com

Matterhorn Nursery
227 Summit Park Road
Spring Valley, NY 10977
(914) 354-5986
www.matterhornnursery.com

Musser Forests, Inc.
Route 119 North
P.O. Box 340
Indiana, PA 15701
(800) 643-8319
(724) 465-5684
www.musserforests.com

Park Seed Company, Inc.
1 Parkton Avenue
Greenwood, SC 29647-001
(800) 845-3369
(864) 223-7333
www.parkseed.com

Roses of Yesterday & Today
803 Brown's Valley Road
Corralitos, CA 95076
(831) 728-1901
www.rosesofyesterday.com

Smith Nursery Co.
P.O. Box 515
Charles City, IA 50616
(641) 228-3239

Stokes Seeds, Inc.
Box 10
Buffalo, NY 14240
(800) 263-7233
www.stokeseeds.com

Thomasville Flower Shop
322 South Broad
Thomasville, GA 31792
(800) 533-4587
(229) 226-3424, 5

Van Engelen, Inc.
Stillbrook Farm
23 Tulip Drive
Bantam, CT 06759
(860) 567-8734
www.vanengelen.com

**Andre Viette Farm
& Nursery**
P.O. Box 1109
Fishersvillle, VA 22939
(800) 575-5538
(540) 943-2315
www.viette.com

**Wavecrest Nursery
& Landscaping Co.**
2509 Lakeshore Drive
Fennville, MI 49408
(616) 543-4175
www.wavecrestnursery.com

Wayside Gardens
1 Garden Lane
Hodges, SC 29695-0001
(800) 845-1124
www.waysidegardens.com

We-Du Nurseries
2055 Polly Spout Road
Marion, NC 28752
(828) 738-8300
www.we-du.com

White Flower Farm
P.O. Box 50
Litchfield, CT 06759
(800) 503-9624
www.whiteflowerfarm.com

Yucca Do Nursery
P.O. Box 907
Hempstead, TX 77445
(979) 826-4580
www.yuccado.com

CANADA

Alberta Nurseries & Seeds
Box 20
Bowden, Alberta
Canada T0M OKO
(403) 224-3544
www.gardenersweb.com

Woodland Nurseries
2151 Camilla Road
Mississauga, Ontario
Canada L5A 2K1
(905) 277-2961
www. eol.ca/~woodland

PAINT AND STAINS

Benjamin Moore & Co.
51 Chestnut Ridge Road
Montvale, NJ 07645
(800) 344-0400
(201) 573-9600
www.benjaminmoore.com

Charrette
31 Olympia Avenue
Woburn, MA 01888
(800) 367-3729
(781) 935-6000
www.charrette.com

Home Depot
10300 Coursey Road
Baton Rouge, LA 70816
(225) 293-9629
www.homedepot.com

Pearl Paint Co.
308 Canal Street
New York, NY 10013
(800) 221-6845
(212) 431-7932
www.pearlpaint.com

Sherwin-Williams Co.
101 Prospect Avenue
Cleveland, OH 44115
(800) 4 SHERWIN
www.sherwin-williams.com

CANADA

Days Painting Supplies
10733 104 Avenue NW
Edmonton, Alberta
Canada TDJ 3KI
(780) 426-4848
www.dayspainting.ab.ca

**Hartmann & Brown Total
Home Interiors**
241 Selby Street
Nanimo, British Columbia
Canada V9R 2R2
(250) 754-2288

New York Paint & Wallpaper
1704 St. Clair Avenue W
Toronto, Ontario
Canada M6N 1J1
(416) 656-2223

**PLANTERS AND
GARDEN STRUCTURES**

Brooklyn Botanic Garden
1000 Washington Avenue
Brooklyn, NY 11225
(718) 623-7200
www.bbg.org

Country Casual
9085 Comprint Court
Gaithersburg, MD 20877
(800) 284-8325
(301) 926-9195
www.countrycasual.com

Gardeners Eden
17 Riverside Street
Nashua, NH 03062
(800) 822-9600

Gardener's Supply Co.
128 Intervale Road
Burlington, VT 05401
(800) 863-1700
(802) 660-3505
www.gardeners.com

Kinsman Co.
6805 Easton Road
P.O. Box 428
Pipersville, PA 18947
(800) 733-4146
www.kinsmangarden.com

Treillage Ltd.
418 East 75th Street
New York, NY 10021
(212) 535-2288

**LUMBER AND BUILDING
SUPPLIES**

Home Depot
449 Roberts Court Road
Kennesaw, GA 30144
(770) 424-1309
www.homedepot.com

Lehigh Portland Cement Co.
7660 Imperial Way
Allentown, PA 18195
(610) 366-4600
www.lehighcement.com

credits

The projects in this book are designed by George Carter except for the following:

Vertical Planting and Wirework Basket (Designer: Jane Seabrook at The Chelsea Gardener).
Much of the planting was lent by John Powles at the Romantic Garden Nursery,
Swannington, Norfolk.

index

acknowledgments

The author would like to thank the many people involved in making

this book: Marianne Majerus, whose photographs make the book so

beautiful; Toria Leitch for editing it; Caroline Davison and Larraine

Shamwana for their help with photo shoots; and Ingunn Jensen for

stylish graphic design. Also John Powles and The Romantic Garden

Nursery for the loan of plants, Jane Seabrook and The Chelsea

Gardener for planting and use of the nursery, and the many people

who have lent their own beautiful gardens as backdrops for

photography: Ethne Clarke, Mrs. David Cargill, Mr. and Mrs. Robert

Clarke, Viscount and Viscountess De L'Isle, Mrs. Clive Hardcastle, The

Lady Tollemache, Mr. and Mrs. Richard Winch, Mr. and Mrs. Derek

Howard, Major Charles Fenwick, Anne Ryland, and Jacqui Small. For

lending urns, thanks to Jill Duchess of Hamilton, for typing, thanks to

Jill Hawer, and for construction and bricklaying to Peter Goodwins

and Jack Bell.